Poetry
is Like
Medicine

Poetry by
Symay Rhodes

WIDER PERSPECTIVES PUBLISHING ¤ NORFOLK, VA. ¤ 2021

Copyright © September 2021, Clifford "Symay" Rhodes
Wider Perspectives Publishing, Norfolk, Va
ISBN: 978-1-952773-44-0

Contents

Medicine

is Like Medicine

... on Bandages

Sometimes poems are like Band-Aids
writing doesn't help
it just seems better than doing nothing
Band-aids don't heal wounds
we use them to cover flaws, I mean scars
so I put a poem things I don't want to say
I put a poem on things I can't talk about
I put a poem on things I can't cry about
I put a poem on the things I argue with God about
I put a poem on the things my brain can't comprehend.
and honestly if I were more focused on the solution...

I would write a poem...

that's more like medicine...

Symay

Ars Poetica #4

Simplify the world
Shapes, Sounds, Textures, Movement
Study the simplicity of lines and grooves
297,342 strokes
of a paint brush
turn blank canvases into artwork
fix senses to blend
smell refined
taste by inhaling
Exhale expectations
only rely on Here
hear the way the music looks
wave, bounce, flatline
how it feels
on skin
surrounded by beauty

Casualties of War

Casualties of war
stacked on bunk beds
tagged 7 and 14
We have been drafted
without asking for a birth certificate
without an age limit
without telling us why
Words sound like bullets sailing through shut doors
        and paper thin walls
pillows don't make good helmets
for hollow bodies filling open ears
creating a hollow feeling in growing bodies
They say bullets don't have names
but these have been engraved
Cheater doesn't sound like mommy
Liar doesn't sound like daddy
Go to your room
my name is not Go To Your Room, Go To Bed, We're Just Talking
Rhodes
but I've felt the hot lead
Because stray bullets never fall on deaf ears
They always bring death to the ones that wished they could drown
out the noise
martyrs die for a purpose
We died because you forgot we had one
Dead bodies don't mourn mornings of eggs, and bacon, and smiles
They just get used to the normalcy of silence
Dead bodies don't wave white flags
they just stop looking out window waiting for the blue pickup truck
        to do what it said it's going to do
        and come back
Why would they call it a pickup truck if you were
        never going to pick us up?
We used to ride in the bed

You fussed at us for doing it
now we lie in bunk beds
debating if it was because it wasn't safe
or you didn't want to open up more space for us
Dead bodies don't read terms of surrender
we just know mommy and daddy split everything in half
Half the crib, half the cash, half the kids,
But it's tough to do the math because we've been
            breaking on the insides for a while now
And were still learning how to divide fractions
Dead bodies don't tell the story of the losing side.
We decompose
wondering who won
who lost
how the hell did we die
when we weren't fighting to begin with.
Now we tend to fight for your attention
like corpses convulsing at a last ditch effort to reach
            the dark end of the tunnel
We were never bad kids
We learned how to fight after
you argued the life out of us
We fight the ones still living because it hurts to see a spitting image
            of what we lost
a happy home is what we lost
sanity is what we lost
a future is what we lost
but at least you won the war.
but what exactly were you fighting for?

Cliche Poem

I am the cliche poet that pulls out the same poem at every open mic
This is a cliche poem
> title
cliche-an overused idea or phrase that lacks original thought
This is the part where I start off slow
This poem is meant to make girls attracted to me
> making sure that I make eye contact with your color contacts
> and later we can exchange contacts so we can keep in contact
This poem tells black people white people suck
This poem takes one poet's poem and protrudes it as a posing poet's
> personal production
I will use many unnecessary literary devices
This poem repeats and rhymes and repeats lines
So it sounds like repeated words are rhymes
This poem
This poem
This poem
This part gets stuck in your head
I will write this in many overused similes that make no sense
Like a round peg going into a square hole
like a round peg going into a triangle hole
like a round peg going into a hole that's not round
This is where the poem builds up
This is where a punch line goes
This is where I speak directly to the judges and try to get them to
> forget about the words in my poem and see the falsified
> emotion in my face
This poem doesn't challenge anything
This poem will not make anyone angry
I did not have to think to write this poem so this poem does not
> make you think
This poem vaguely talks about buzz words everyone knows about to
> make you think we made a connection

Columbine, 9/11, Rodney King, Swine flu, Iraq,
Katrina, Trump, Walls, Gender

I will name people and quotes to make you believe I am very
        knowledgeable
                Malcolm, Plymouth rock, Martin, the dream,
                Dickinson, Frost, hope is a thing with feathers,
                        the road not taken

This is the poem's climax

This is where I say some thing that makes sense
But it's so convoluted you don't comprehend it until
        twenty minutes later
                so you think it was cool
This is where I slow everything down
This is the part where I tell you everything I just told you
        in one simple line
This where I walk off and hope I inspired something meaningful
Something you've never heard before

Explaining Depression to Friends

(to Sabrina Beniam)

Explaining depression to friends is like instantly
        becoming a 3 year old
lost in the middle of a mall
Excessive amounts of stares
as if you all of a sudden
are out of place
when seconds before no one would look your way

no one really knows what to say
they just look
afraid
I don't know how it feels but I'd imagine it's like
        your best friend telling you they're gay
"You're not depressed"
"You like life"
"I know you're not depressed, I've seen you being happy"
well being in the closet for me
is staying in bed until 3
hoping and praying just to go back to sleep
solitary drinking games with nothing to eat
hoping for starvation or dehydration because
I'm too afraid to make myself bleed
and God somewhere watching
with his own agenda
prayers returned to sender
if any man diminishes my cross to bear
I got a few splinters to lend him
Each step is a trip to the gates of hell
tempted to stick my foot in.

Explaining depression to friends
is like instantly becoming a 3 year old
lost in the middle of a mall
Excessive amounts of stares

as if you all of a sudden
are out of place
when seconds before no one
would look your way
rapid fire questions that you don't all the way
      know the answers to

"Where do you live" home
"Where is home" I don't know
"Why don't you know" I don't know

it's not that I don't, but it's hard explaining
that if home is where the heart is
bits and pieces left a long time ago
Nia has my front door somewhere at A&T
Danielle and Monique took my basement and
      my foundation-shaking further relationships
a few in between took the windows
Each nailed a board to the empty spaces
so I can't see past the moment they left
all I have is my room with Posters and Pictures
      of Family and Friends
and the ink in this pen
but portraits fade and are accidentally dumped
      like well wishes,
        and one girl floats in and out
riding her fingers up and down my guitar
I wonder if she knows where she is.
so I don't spend too much time where my heart is
when roaming my mind is more soothing and less confusing

Explaining depression to friends
is like instantly becoming a 3 year old
lost in the middle of a mall
Excessive amounts of stares
as if you all of a sudden are out of place
rapid fire questions that you don't all the way know
      the answer to

and everyone wants to hold your hand, tell you it will be okay,
            and point you in the right direction

but when everyone tells me the same thing
friend, Enemies, those that overheard the private conversation,
            or hearing this poem say the same thing
it really sounds like bullshit
friends tell the truth but lie to save your feelings
Enemies lie but tell the truth to hurt your feelings
so who's lying to me?
and an empty room is still an empty room
a crowded room of friends is still an empty room
just with less space to move
blank faces like chess pieces
moving in different directions
all trying to check on me
and I hate all of you for it
and I thank you

Explaining depression to friends
is like instantly becoming a 3 year old lost in the middle of a mall

one person says the right thing and it feels like mom found me
right next to Aunt Annie's
Eating a pretzel
and I forgot why I was there in the first place
your "How are you?" is that awkward hug when
            you first meet a person
it feels so nice that it's uncomfortable
outwardly you don't want anyone to touch you
but inwardly you need something to hold on to.
so piss me off to the point I'm not mad at life anymore
make not living a lot harder than living is
and somebody pray
just pray
because one of these days he'll be right on time

He Lays There Undead

He lays there undead
Corpse carved across his forehead
Life leaking from embalmment eager lips
The imprint of ribs rest on his abdomen
Like chalk lines on pavement
When did notebook paper white become a flesh tone
Alone
He is connected to a wall
Tied to a machine
Fighting for his last breath
Without a stool in his corner
Monitors spike like stalactites
The light at the end of his tunnel
Is yet dim
Statuesque
Sunken in the mattress
Like half buried debris
If a man is in pain
But is not aware to feel it
Does it really hurt
Lost connected to a wall
Tied to a machine
Fighting for his last seconds
Without a soul in his corner
Suction cups
Relay his journey to a screen
While sowing his feet to reality
I can hear him
"cut this noose
Allow me to sleep"
David's finger within reach
Break him free from his wall
Lift him from his wall
I pray to the Lord
His soul to keep

Clay on a Canvas

Like a painter clumsily handling clay like pastel paints
I'm learning this art form might not be for me
The picture up here is shot in 8k quality
microscopic zoom
and the hues boom
make it feel front row to the running movie of my imagination.
But from here to your ears
it doesn't always translate correctly
like idioms from an immigrant
the picture isn't clear
moving the antenna
but there's static in my schools of thought
my thoughts academically should be filtered on the page through
dismissing phrases that don't add to meaning
edit, critique, revise, rewrite
don't rhyme all the time
flip a cliche on its head
or maybe on its toes
a universal you isn't universal
unless you is the only name you have to address you
use an economy of words
spend vocabulary
like dollars right before rent is due
every letter has too much value in this house
be concrete let them see the emotion
in the imagery
don't tell me how to feel
don't tell me anything
Show me
lines don't end at line breaks
from writing help you forget your emotional attachment before
evaluation
remember your punctuation
Punk u ain't grow up rhyming like that

slowing down lines. you pausing for snaps?
write bars that hit hard like pipes packed with crack
spit punchlines that make your face curl up like that
Do it 'cuz it sounds hood like sound would
Waste a line 'cuz it rhymes and that sounds good
kill it like hearin' KKK rollin' with the grim reaper in Arizona with
skittles
You gotta sound hood
You wrote it how you meant it
don't cut words out
you got sixteen bars
give 8 written then freestyle in and out
Your flow is fluid don't bottle it
nastier than zombie spit
just beyond common sense
clean as a fresh out of the laundry fit
just empty the whole clip
or not
Sometimes there's a middle ground
I'm still trying to find it.
when I'm writing
Where's the plus sign and where's the minus
see that rhyme was a little forced too.
I'm just a painter
Trying to place clay on a canvas the right way
making memories that feel like movies feel the same way to you.
making statements that dream like reality feel real to you too.

The #9 bus

The #9 bus
Gets crushed by change
In the same way it came
Daily
Cigarette smokes bless throats
And float together

An Ode to Cedar Grove

there won't a whole lot of Cedars
at Cedar Grove
there used to be
but the buses came
then there was just a lot of tree
and these simplistic negroes askin' and harassin' me
You smoke?
I got that loud pack 2 for 15
Dirty hands exchange cash in a flash
Cops roll past
Dope boys laugh and get lost
In the hustle and buses of Cedar Grove
And the old heads stationed to sell they cigarettes
1 for 35, 2 for 50 and 3 for a dollar
These cats move weight

Shorties chase the bus
Dudes chase below the waist
Or at least catch a glance
Pockets full of change
Can not be wasted
$1.50 to get me home
$3.00 to work and back
And $5.50 to get me to the beach
I sho don't go to the beach

I just creep along
as those buses do
in that unusual, uncanny amount of time
it takes for that #9
to get to Cedar Grove
but they moved the bus station
my haven
my saving grace
across the street from the church

no longer can these street entrepreneurs lurk
for pigs are out
ready to fly
If you are out at this transit center
Selling your soul
 Like they did at Cedar Grove
They will send you south for the winter
And you won't make it back home
Imprisoned in open space
I miss my Grove.

is Like Medicine

... on Casts

Sometimes poems feel like casts
letting you know something is broken
but protecting the fragile pieces
everyone wants to sign the cast
but no one ever checks to see if the bone is setting right
people will ask you when is the cast coming off
but never ask you if it still hurts
people will ask you to perform the poem
but they never ask you if it still hurts
people will ask why the cast
people will ask why the poem
both are just exposition to an entertaining story...

Princess Tiana Got a Job

Princess Ariel traded her voice
to meet a man who couldn't love her as she was
Belle was kidnapped
and succumbed to Stockholm syndrome with an abusive thug
Snow White and Sleeping Beauty were sexually assaulted in their sleep
Woke up to love at first creep
Got married and we assume they lived happily ever after because
they never made a peep
They had aspirations of being arm candy
and were cradled in kingdoms
never having to lift a finger again...

Princess Tiana was turned into an amphibian
had some man child slither in to a plan
more manual than magic
He needed a mother more than a wife
she was traveled in a swamp
with a gator and firefly
that never turned in to horses like
the white mice
she found love being stuck
she married a frog prince
with a frog wife
she had settled for a frog life
and what was her reward
for finding love in contentment
a job
a promotion and entrepreneurship
an opportunity to pay taxes and get screwed a bit
The other princesses were paid taxes
privilege at its finest
How does it feel to be carried to safety
and be called your highness

Tiana faced the eyes of death
and fought back
not only being a damsel in distress, but assisting in her own rescue
that whole part Snow White and Aurora slept through
Tiana did all of that
to become middle class
with a prince with no kingdom husband
who can finally chop onions
It's New Orleans, USA
only the king is dumb enough
to think he reigns over a parade
keep believing in fairy tales
because there's still
a backseat in happily ever after

Jesus in a Laundromat
(Matt-25:30)

I met Jesus in a laundromat
He was pulling my clothes out of a machine
It had obviously been a while since He had on something clean
The clothes He wore were so worn
the South Pole had turned North
This might be the closest thing to Christmas
since He was born
But your average obese Caucasian male
would not be dressed in jolly red
but instead police blues
And be disgusted by Jesus's presence on park benches
rather than leaving a present
under the tree
where He can get it.
Santa don't exist where Jesus lives

But He gifted himself a shirt two sizes too big
It looked like my sin
He didn't deserve it
but he carried like it was perfectly tailored
He traded in his pants which had scraped holes at the knees
It was not fashion they were fashioned
by him praying for his father
"if it is at all possible don't take this cup from Me"
It's My only hope for change and
I thirst
for change

Jesus put on a pair of jeans
it looked like for a moment they counteracted His genes
poverty passed down for generations
This seems like the God of Adam, Abraham and David,
the one He thought had forsaken Him
had finally sewn Him in seam

of the jeans out the machine
but they saw Him
and they stopped him
cuffed him with cross expressions
looking him up and down
without reaching across
crucifixion in their faces
all because the clothes weren't His

I said, "I'm sorry, these clothes are mine.
Can you please let Him live?
You crucified Him once can we not do this again?"
This is Salvation in the flesh
He died so I can live
a little of myself is the least that I can give
I looked at Jesus and said, "Take what You want."
and if you're hungry let's break bread
The wine on his breath was evidence of bloodshed
The people in the laundromat looked at me like I was crazy
"This is no king, he's just dirty and lazy.
He'll never change."
I simply said, "A miracle happened 2000 years ago
that most wouldn't believe

It could happen again."

Where's Moses

Tell old, Pharoh
Let my people go

Even while being raised as an Egyptian
Moses killed a man for excessively
beating a Hebrew slave
Probably didn't know either man's name but he knew
that wasn't
right
things had to change
took care of the problem
Nothing was the Same
just because of a simple conviction.
Dear God,
Where was Moses in Fruitvale Station on New Year's Day 2009?
Egyptian Bart officer pounding a new age slave
named Oscar Grant.
nominated for an Oscar but Granted his death.
do we only get one Moses per life?
or has earth just changed.
was he sleep when Trayvon was beat?
or are we the Egyptian descendants getting what we deserve.
Do we do our own dirt so much Zimmermann ain't know that
him killing us and us killing us ain't equal?
Did he say I come from the great I Am and we ask
is He C.O.G.I.C, Pentecostal, or Baptist
did he look like 2Chains or Randy Travis
I seen prince of Egypt part two is in effect.

Where's Moses of Alexander street
getting kicked out of Ghent
seeing God on the burning TV
telling him
drop his chain so it turns to a Glock that loads with the 41 bullet

that got Amadou Dialo shot
turn overpriced narcotics to a 40 ounce and a blunt?
What do you do when your medicine is made illegal?

Infest Congress' steps with Louisiana Mosquitoes
 and Brooklyn Rats
but they might be used to being around vermin
or maybe God will strike down every first born bigot
then we split this red sea of wealth right down the middle
or did I miss it.

Did Ms. Tubman get us to the wilderness
where we could hold our own?
Brother Martin and Brother Malcolm gave the commands
to show us how to get home
but we moan and groaned for 400 years.
Maybe Joshua is the one who's not here
Moses led the slaves out of shackles
Joshua led the slaves out of complacency
so with every fear of, laced weed
cops chasing me
everything due on the 1st and the 15th
and every other ghetto stereotype you can attach to me.
I know that the Jericho surrounding my peace is mental
and the seventh trumpet blow is near

so to complacency
to apathy
to fear
to tradition
to opinionated fiction portrayed as news
to anger
to pride

I tell my ego
Let my people go

Professor Overseer
- A Riot is The Language of the Unheard

Professor Overseer
With tenure sitting in his lap
Like shotgun pointed at HBCU students
He finds the necessity to benevolently teach the difference between
                                    Negro, Nigra, and Nigger
to define Ruins as Baltimore after Freddie Gray
to say Baltimore the same way you say Nigger
Saying you just can't understand
why people would destroy their own city.
Damn, I think he called me a Nigger
I said calmly with balled fist
I'm from there, It's not ruined it's just weeping
He went on
I replied that's my city, it don't look that way.
I couldn't get any louder than a whisper
I guess I was trying to keep that Nigger in my voice sleeping
To make sure that Nigra stayed in line
To make sure the Negro didn't grow black enough
                                    to have to apologize
Understand, A riot is the language of the unheard
And you are playing with fire in this Classroom
Baltimore ignored the cries of its beating heart
Thinking its blood beat blue wearing Ku Klux undergarments
But, instead it bleed black so much
that when Black blood hit the streets
it wasn't out of the usual
So they had to put black on cars they couldn't see themselves drive
The had to put black on business that wouldn't
                                    serve their community
They had to put black on blue uniforms because
                                    they were tired of heart attacks
The thing on the inside that is supposed to be keeping you alive
keeps beating and beating and beating

Until it stops.

Ruins are the state of being disintegrated
A city that cares nothing for its people is in ruins
A city that leaves a twenty five year old man to rot in a van is in ruins
The city was in ruins before April 2015
The people just wanted the outside to match the inside
so don't blame Freddie
It's the fault of people like Professor Overseer
who was this close to having a classroom in ruins

7th Grade Caucasian Female

I asked you to have a seat.

You said..."No"
and with that I heard this imaginary slap
that had been etched in my brain with every look in the mirror
Because my mother reminded me that the black on my skin
                                                    was removable

I said, I'm sorry I didn't greet you,
I know I'm not your normal teacher,
I'm a sub who's really glad to meet you.
can you please have a seat?
You said..."No"
Not an I dont want to, or do I have to.
But, a casual...no
You were hiding behind two desks
Annoying two students
and Affecting two of my nerves
Plucking the first while getting on my last one
I made a plea trying to sell you on obedience
                                with a sales pitch of common sense.
I didn't disrespect you, so don't disrespect me.
There's an order to this classroom for us to begin
Your classmates waiting for the logic bus to arrive
it obviously missed its stop
You staged a one person boycott of History class when I reused
                                to get angry or raise my voice.
The privilege in your walk irritated my melanin
Security brought you back
where you refused to sit in you assigned seat

Be glad you have the privilege of saying no.
Be glad that my patience is not racially motivated

The girl next door has a brother facing life today
The teacher asked her to read out loud
She shut down like the life she was holding had become too heavy.
She was strong enough to not look weak
while folding inside from a head-on collision
between fear and apathy
Her teacher didn't give her a pass on her attitude
                         that passed after a heart to heart.
she kicked her out
and let security pick her up for skipping class
And her brain skips the steps to cope with stress
and security skips steps of de-escalation
when she just needed to decompress
They skip her straight to referral
referred her to the next not-my-problem adult
that looks a lot like the way her mama looked at her brother
before they handcuffed him

be glad you have the privilege of saying no

Because if you looked like me,
security would have removed you from class
                        before I picked up the phone to call
Security would have asked you for an ID for walking down the hall
Security would have told you to assume the position
                        in front of your locker
Opened it because of the suspicious smell
Dumped your belongings on the floor
                        and tell you to pick them up as well
as soon as you reach for your scissors or your pen.
It could even be an eraser
it doesn't matter to them
Guns are drawn
They say don't move she's armed
and dangerous
with the opportunity of an education
don't wait for her to grow up

is Like Medicine

If she grows she'll learn
then the tables will turn
some of them will actually be afraid of the books in your hands
others just want to see you squirm

The moment you look like you want to walk
                                out of this awkward class
                        with experience as its only teacher
darkened skin as your only distinguishing feature
                        and your life held at the end of an index finger

I bet you'd wish you could have said no.

10 Things I Would Say
to My Unborn Son

1. Daddy will always be here

2. Sometimes in life there will be things you don't understand
Chess positions you won't find in a book
so every move looks like a mistake

3. Adults make mistakes
things that we regret
glasses of spilled milk we wished we never poured

4. You are not a mistake
The thought of you has brought me more joy
than it will ever bring pain
I am sorry
that the thought of you will ever bring pain

5. Adults are not always as strong as you need us to be
Daddy wasn't as strong as mommy needed him to be
Daddy couldn't carry you as long as you needed to get here
If I could, I would
but I couldn't
Mommy was strong enough to make her choice
there is a difference between
being selfish and self-preservation
Mommy has to be strong enough
to carry the weight of both
If Daddy had his way
Daddy would take the earth from Atlas
drink the Atlantic
until he uncovered Atlantis
just to see your toes could touch the ground

but sometimes wonders of the world are only
remembered after you drown

6. Daddy won't always be upset at mommy
She just forgot to tell me you were here
I know you didn't mean to make her late
I wish she didn't see you as the thing holding her up
I'm sorry I never got the pleasure of holding you up
I'm sorry I was praying with closed eyes and folded hands so instead
of reaching out to yours
God filled the difference between infancy and deity started hoisting
you up

7. Say what's up to God
If you make it up there
You were never born to be born again
I wonder if you had a soul to be saved from sin
If you make it up there
Ask him for his tips on losing a child that did nothing wrong
Now, I understand
Your heavenly body is hereditary
She was supposed to be my world
but she eclipsed my sun
so she will forever be my moon
and nothing in my soul or system
is sitting right.

8. You have a purpose
people will tell you that you are worthless
They just aren't willing to pay for something perfect
just the way it is
They will always choose themselves over you
If it would help, I would give up myself over you
You are a mountain the size of a mole hill
and there is no getting over you

9. People keep telling me you never existed
But, If that's true why was there a trip to the clinic
I planned for parenthood
but my choice was never there to begin with.

10. Daddy is still here

Breast Cancer

Walking in to my mother's bedroom
Where beds creep up and down like children after midnight
And more cords connect to limp bodies than to television sets
Where life has hit that awkward pause in conversation
And death has signed for a visitors badge
And this sick feeling
Is Peeling away at a future you dreamed up as a child
Because no little girl
Said I want to watch my children grow up from a hospital bed
And watch legs atrophy from lacking the energy
                                        to pick them up in the morning.
No little girl prays for a bald and broken
                            chemotherapy barbie for Christmas
                            and says I wanna be just like her
No little girl asks for the image of beauty her future husband
                    finds the day they met to be as temporary
                            as wedding ring pops
No little girl wishes that her outside
                        makes it hard for him to keep loving her
                                        on the inside
Because it is her insides that are killing her
                    and nothing on the outside is fighting back
Her outer beauty kept in photo albums
                        and the remnants of 30 hiding
                            in her face, in her cheeks
                        foundation of hopes and dreams
Cling to tongue and cheek
Well wishes and Bible scriptures
But no little girl prayed Thy Will be done
And expected to be left hanging
Dying to do his will
In her will
Still wondering if God
Still cares

Still stands or
Stands still
While she can't stand up
She dreamed of singing on stages,
Instead of being stuck on stage 5
Stage one
This one I plant my feet on
And distribute words
Like vaccinations that don't exist
Stage two
Is two feet one in front of the other
Taking every step my mother won't see on earth
Making each imprint dent the earth the same size
                         you imprinted my heart

Stage three is not this no not this
Stage four is Bullshit too much for me to handle.
                         And it's spreading

And stage 5 is acceptance
Stage 5 is accept this
Stage 5 is anything except this
Stage 5 is four fingers down to anyone
                    who thinks I should accept this.

Now you're
Gone with an open end
And I'm living, trying
To be the son
You prayed

is Like Medicine

... on Novocaine

Sometimes poems feel like Novocain
numbing pain until it's edible
easily digestible
3 minute pieces
but real pain is a pill
not easy to swallow
real pain stays lodged in your throat
like choking
on your own tongue
so you can't call for help
like dry heaving on yourself
thinking there is more of you
that has to come out
but nothing ever actually comes out
real pain is like a false alarm for death
this is only a drill but now
you know what's it feels like
when your heart stops
because poems just press pause on the pain

then pain presses play on reality...

To Every Girl at Cookout's
Drive Thru Window

You are beautiful
To a point of contempt
Just for the simple fact that your service
Is the smile I want from Walmart greeters
Instead of the dentures riding the after taste of prune juice
Baby you smell like burgers and milkshakes
And on our 1st date
After you get off work
I'll take you out
To my kitchen
So it will smell like food is actually made there
Your service is undeniable wonderful
I think
If you got my order wrong
You're too beautiful for me to remember
You always remember a straw and a spoon with my
Chocolate chip cookie dough, strawberry cheesecake shake
And only forgot the Cajun on my fries one time
You're the only one to give me chicken nuggets as a side
AS A SIDE!!!
McDonald's has those can I take your order
Middle Aged manager mini-van moms with no kids
And a nugget meal that cost like $7
Cookout drive thru window girl
I love you like a double burger
Holding both buns like your buns
But actually, I've never seen below that window
So I'll love your top half
As long as it brings me my order

Coffee (A.E.)

She walked in American Lit 384
fragrant of Folgers and high fashion
hinting of chocolate
her skin
caramel mocha cappuccino
venti skinny body
She speaks in Starbucks
sprinkled with Suffolk suburb
but she's filled
with substance
no milk, no cream
black brewed
back of the conscious book store bitter
aromatherapy at quarter after nine
unattached my nose from this textbook spine
reading romantic writers on pages
promoting heaven in nature
I found an Angel in a natural
her caffeine
keeps me wide awake
in a daydream
that we could
take a short walk
to the student union
3 floors up
and grab a cup
of a long conversation

Shorty Do Wop
(a response)

I love making short jokes
About you specifically
Not to be mean
I like the way your nose wrinkles
And your voice
When you sound irritated
It's slightly weird
A rollercoaster of pitches
Lifted until your voice is as tall
As wish you were
You slap at my arm and back
With a smile
Like "don't point out my imperfections
And make me love them"
But I love the top of your head
and the space your head rest
when you hug me
don't grow
so far
that I can't love you the way I'm accustomed to.

Tower of Babel (A.E.)

God split the tongues of man
because the Tower of Babel
stood so close
its measurements
rivaled heavenly dimensions
I wonder...

Is that the reason I can never find
the right phrase
to communicate the heaven
in your skin
the wings which arch your back
 the gates holding grace
behind the brown in each iris
the freshly twisted out halo
held in a rubber band
wine colored from the last supper
the tower of each leg and the stairway to God in each arm
reach this upper room conversation
with myself...

This will be death
translating shyness, quiet, a hibernating panic
to "let us build closer to Heaven together"
but the tongues of man only stretch so far
it makes sense
to keep gold paved streets
neatly tucked
at a conversation's length
if God's most famous words have been written by man
this poem is an ice breaking prayer
placed in God's hands...

"Hello"

Could I Ask You a Question?

Wait, I just did?
But that's not what I wanted to ask you.
How do I ask you a question?
Wait, that's not the question.
What should I ask you?
No that's not the question either.
Why is this so hard?
No, that's not the question.

Stop

If I could have just a moment of time
to ask your number and name and maybe your age
and what page of this unfinished manuscript
of the last book of the bible we're walking in is your favorite.
Would you change it?
What would you name it?
Would we go back to being naked,
stripped bare before God on the eve of history?
What is your version of this story?
Who's the Judas that switched the colors on your rubix cube?
That made life more of a puzzle than it was supposed to be?
Would you read it vocally,
paint it visually,
dance out each word like footsteps sounding out syllables?
Would you ignore my ignorant intellect?
And respect the simplicity of wisdom
And when I say something so dumb
that it seems like my brain got into a fight with my tongue
So bad they're not talking to each other.
You laugh it off like it was a joke, but I kinda meant it
Would you hold me accountable?
But not keep count of my transgressions
Would you cook for me?

What are you cooking?
How are you doing?
What are you doing later?

Specifically, the later part of forever
Or maybe Tomorrow night
How does that sound?
Is that right?
Wait, I know

Can I ask you more questions?

One Flesh

GEN 2:24 A man leaves his father and mother
and joins with his wife to become one flesh

I want a love that's definite
Love your wives like Christ loved the church
So there's gotta be death in it
Die daily as our walks converge on living water
All else we can deafen it
I ain't trying to have your best friends relationship
I'm trying to build our own thing then strengthen it
Take all of your past pain and strangle it
Every bad memory and mangle it
Until it only reminds you how far we came
I'm trying to love you like my walk loves my big toe
Without you I'm Awkward, unbalanced, bound to fall.
But it looks okay
because my shoes still fit.
I wanna love you like a ball and chain
Keep me anchored where I'm supposed to be
Leaving you might mean cutting off a piece of me
I'm trying to love you like my tongue loves the roof of my mouth
The way my diction dictates
the art of the griot
passed down through the ages
generation to generation
Just to tell the story of you
And at the end
My lips can only preach an amen
Because I'm thankful
Like my lisp
If I could list every way I could love you
Number 22 would be
I want to love you as much as I hate the s in the word lisp
And any other word with an s sound
I wanna love you as much as I like you
I wanna like like you

like sandbox, slapbox, playhouse Disney out of the box
like passing notes in class
leaving notes in your locker
singing notes off key
giving you a key that don't go to nothing
but sayin something sappy like it goes to my heart
I wanna love you more than relationship goals
more than Beyonce and Jay Z
I wanna love you a life longer than JoJo and K-ci
More than 70's R&B
I wanna love you like that Lenny Williams song
I, I, I wanna love you so much I stutter, sing and cry at the same time
I wanna love you until television goes off

I wanna love you 13 reasons more than your situation
more than chemo
more than repo
more than no shows
more than logos
more than log ins
more than passwords
more than unheard
more than blind herds
more than kind words
more than well wishes
more than 5 loaves and two fishes and a chicken biscuit
more than Chik-fil-a service
more than water and wifi
more than hell you're in
I wanna love you in what God hasn't brought you through yet
I wanna love you to what God has planned for you,
but haven't gotten to yet
I wanna love you so much I can't wait to see what's next
2 become 1
Let no man put asunder

is Like Medicine

... on Medicine

I would write a poem
that's more like medicine
addressing the issue
would lead to redressing the bandage
identifying the pain
would lead to prescribing a poem
performing it on stage for 3-4 weeks
and if the pain still persists

maybe someone else's has stopped
because poems are like medicine
but poets are not patients
they are doctors
who happen to self-medicate sometimes

Searching

Searching
for faith
between white pages with
black letters of
brown faces
under mounds
of fiction written
in invisible ink.
I found it
cradled next to the truth
Attempting to stay warm
until the sun rises
again

I've Been Changed

"I know I've been changed
Angels in heaven done signed my name"

Change: Verb. to make different
synonym. to alter

to make change a dollar has to be broken
to fit a suit, the material has to be altered
so, are you willing to break at the altar?
to find this change you're suited for
or do you want to alter the altar
so you bend but don't break
in places that clearly don't fit together?
Is your faith fabricated
only activated by what makes you comfortable
still sleeping in pjs when God called for fatigues?
Oh you fatigued?, you tired?, ready to retire?
trying to tread lightly?
When God says go I'm rolling 'til I need to re-tire
run, and not grow weary
walk, and not grow faint
The Lord can take my yoke over, easy
The decision of submission is tough to make
This ain't magic, I'll take the harder way
no penny
I'll take the nicks and bruises along the way
It cost more over on the cross anyway
I'm diametrically opposed to things that ain't God
I'll drip my sixth quart of blood
before I ever turn back the other way
but you ain't trying to change

Luke warm
You ain't ready to pull at bad stitching when it's falling apart
I'd rather cut off the sleeve to save the shirt

9th chapter, Book of Mark
ignoring holes in your walk instead of walking holy
Scared to take off sin
it's cool if it happens slowly
I've been there leaning on my own understanding
Wondering why I can't do right when I try
so hard to keep reaching
someone keeps raising the bar
before I leaned on God
change didn't make sense
like selling the house trying to pay the rent
but letting God remake you
that's change well spent
Change:
It's messy
makes a lot of noise when you walk with it.
You have to break what you thought was whole,
but after a while of correct change
you'll realize how much you've saved,
and it adds up to so much more

I know I've been changed.

Star Player

5 foot 6
glasses made thick
before Russell Westbrook made it fashion sense.
As a church boy, I try to stay abstinent
so there's a lot of speculation on the team I'm with.
Well, the Son is at the guard
because he took the charge.
When he died on the cross
the sins were ours.
Holy Spirit is at the 4, the power forward
He moves through us to push the power forward
The Father is at the center
because things go through Him.
Satan comes at me
Mutombo wag that sin.
He's at the 1 and the 3
because He's 3-in-1.
I can sit on the bench
waiting for my chance to come.
He took Short-and-nerdy
to an all-star team.
Now I can slay any giant with the sling.
And that team that you were speculating,
I'm on the straight one.
Straight to the king.

This Telephone Pole

This telephone pole, wood stripped, a towering figure
It reminded me of Jesus, only
His nails were bigger

It reminded me of Him, broken and injured
Dying slowly
The telephone pole wood stripped, a towering figure

Pierced his side through his stomach and liver
He rested there coldly,
But His nails were bigger

Our connections to the cross are like handcuffs for fingers
Holding me
Like the telephone pole wood stripped, a towering figure

Looking at this pole in the dead of winter
Stapled, cut, bug, moldy
But, His nails were bigger

Hearts become tender
I wonder, if and when I get to heaven, will it be what I expected,
and will he notice me?
Like that telephone pole wood stripped, a towering figure
But, His nails were bigger

Superpowered

When I take these glasses off
I don't turn into Superman.
But, when I close my eyes tight
I walk by faith in a super man
who went through the world
showed God in His walk
when they put the Iron in Him
He rose like Tony Stark.

My God got a wrath
that put Hulk in anger management.
He's so incredible
He's the one who makes the planet spin.
Take him for granted
then you're robbing Him
I give him what he asks for
He's Batman, I'll Robin Him.

Even when people are Two-faced
without being burned by acid
He'll still wrap His arms around you
like He's Mr. Fantastic.
I'm not the one
shooting lasers out my glasses
but I will X man
and follow God with a passion.

SportsCenter
(Angels sing Dunna Dun, Dunna Dun)

Two most consistent things in life
SportsCenter   & God

2 AM home from drunken nights
grammatically innovating text messages
All while the Call,   Ringing

ignored by highlights
yellow, blue and white
Klay
drops 37 repetitive rain drops
Proof that God came down, stopped
And rose for 12 minutes in the 3rd
All while The Call,   Ringing

Post-Game Interviews, Posterizing Immortalizing Dunks and Dimes
Post bail for DUI, After posting tweets
                        postpone picking up The Call

I'm Afraid
I'm trying to audibly act like I didn't hear The Call
not easily Accepted. I'm trying to find Jonah's script
running pressed in my flesh. looking for the right decision
questioning Coach
        don't put me in
        I ain't ask to play
        I'll stick to Practice on Sunday
        not a life.
        that Jesus died for.
        but Practice.
but there's an Angel somewhere preaching
"And the Lord said you've got to rise up! Holla/lujah"

3 AM, God's here
and He's been leaving Voicemails on my television
I'm sobering up
clutching this phone
      okay I'll forward The Message

is Like Medicine

Poetry is Like Medicine

Sometimes poems feel like Novocain
numbing pain until it's edible
easily digestible
3 minute pieces
but real pain is a pill
not easy to swallow
real pain stays lodged in your throat
like choking
on your own tongue
so you can't call for help
like dry heaving on yourself
thinking there is more of you
that has to come out
but nothing ever actually comes out
real pain is like a false alarm for death
this is only a drill but now
you know what's it feels like
when your heart stops
because poems just press pause on the pain
then pain presses play on reality

Sometimes poem feel like casts
letting you know something is broken
but protecting the fragile pieces
everyone wants to sign the cast
but no one ever checks to see if the bone is setting right
people will ask you when is the cast coming off
but never ask you if it still hurts
people will ask you to perform the poem
but they never ask you if it still hurts

is Like Medicine

people will ask why the cast
people will ask why the poem
both are just exposition to an entertaining story

Sometimes poems are like band-aids
writing doesn't help
it just seems better than doing nothing
band-aids don't heal wounds
we use them to cover flaws I mean scars
so I put a poem things I don't want to say
I put a poem on things I can't talk about
I put a poem on things I can't cry about
I put a poem on the things I argue with God about
I put a poem on the things my brain can't comprehend.
and honestly if I were more focused on the solution

I would write a poem
that's more like medicine
addressing the issue
would lead to redressing the bandage
identifying the pain
would lead to prescribing a poem
performing it on stage for 3-4 weeks
and if the pain still persists

maybe someone else's has stopped
because poems are like medicine
but poets are not patients
they are doctors
who happen to self-medicate sometimes

colophon

Brought to you by Wider Perspectives Publishing, care of J. Scott Wilson, with the mission of advancing the poetry and creative community of Hampton Roads, Virginia.
See our production of works from ...

Edith Blake
Tanya Cunningham-Jones
Taz Weysweete' (Scientific Eve)
Terra Leigh
Ray Simmons
Samantha Borders-Shoemaker
Bobby K.
(The Poor Man's Poet)
J. Scott Wilson (TEECH!)
Charles Wilson
Gloria Darlene Mann
Neil Spirtas
Zach Crowe
Jorge Mendez & JT Williams
Sarah Eileen Williams
Stephanie Diana (Noftz)
the Hampton Roads
Artistic Collective

Jason Brown (Drk Mtr)
Martina Champion
Tony Broadway
Ken Sutton
Crickyt J. Expression
Lisa M. Kendrick
Cassandra IsFree
Nich (Nicholis Williams)
Samantha Geovjian Clarke
Natalie Morison-Uzzle
Gus Woodward II
Patsy Bickerstaff
Catherine TL Hodges
Jack Cassada
Chichi Iwuorie

... and others to come soon.

We promote and support the artists of the 757
from the seats, from the stands,
from the snapping fingers and
clapping hands
from the pages, and the stages
and now we pass them forth
to the ages

Check for the above artists on FaceBook, the Virginia Poetry Online channel on YouTube, and other social media.

Hampton Roads Artistic Collective is charitable extension of WPP which strives to simultaneously support worthy causes in Hampton Roads and the local creative artists.

Made in the USA
Middletown, DE
02 March 2023